SIERRA
sierra mountain flowers

by

millie miller

Johnson Books
Boulder

Sierra Star Tulip
calochortus minimus
lily   4-8"
a very low flower
that blooms in moist
mountain meadows

Mariposa Lily
calochortus leichtlinii
lily   8-16"
an early spring butterfly
of open clearings
and woods

Fivespot
nemophilia maculata
water leaf   3-12"
delightful little bowls
that bloom early in
foothill meadows

Bistort
polygonum bistortoides
buckwheat   8-12"
a puff of cotton
from wet meadows
to rocky slopes

Washington Lily
lilium washingtonianum
lily   2-6'
this fragrant 'shasta lily'
prefers dry forests...
grows purple with age

Chickweed
cerastium arvense
pink   4-12"
a little 'mouse ear' that
scampers over moist
rocky slopes in
early spring

MarshMarigold

caltha leptosepala
buttercup   6-12"
   blooms as the snow
melts in wet
      mountain marshes

Solomon's Seal

smilacina stellata
lily   1-2'
   an early 'lily of the
   valley' that hides
   in moist places

Shinleaf

pyrola picta
wintergreen   4-12"
   fragrant waxy
   flowers of
   shady forests

Jimson Weed
datura meteloides
nightshade 2-5'
a dazzling vine that
turns blue & closes at
day's end

Bear Grass
xerophyllum tenox
lily 1-5'
flowers every 5-7 years
in low woods and
meadows

Popcorn Flower
plagiobothrys nothofulvus
borage 6-24"
little white puffs that
carpet low meadows
in early spring

SALLY

Cut-leaved Daisy

erigeron compositus
composite 8-12"
favors dry areas...
many daisy
relatives

Monument Plant

frasera speciosa
gentian 2-5'
'deers-tongue'
grows tall on open
mountain slopes

Alpine Gentian

gentiana newberryi
gentian 1-5"
a tiny flower that
hides in alpine
meadows

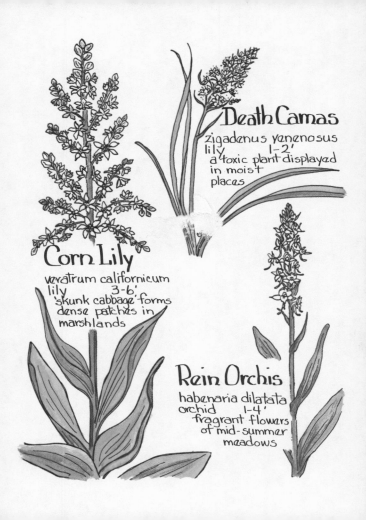

Death Camas
zigadenus venenosus
lily   1-2'
a toxic plant displayed
in moist
places

Corn Lily
veratrum californicum
lily   3-6'
'skunk cabbage' forms
dense patches in
marshlands

Rein Orchis
habenaria dilatata
orchid   1-4'
fragrant flowers
of mid-summer
meadows

Ranger's Button

sphenosciadium capitellatum
carrot   2-5'
bright knobs
of mountain
streams and
marshes

Cow Parsnip

heracleum lanatum
carrot   3-8'
a large showy plant
found in moist
mountain meadows

Yarrow

achillea lanulosa
composite   1-3'
achilles reportedly used
this as medicine for
his soldiers' wounds

Columbine

aquilegia pubescens
buttercup   6-30"
  delicate bloom of rocky
  slopes and windy
  mountain passes
  ...also red

Prickly Poppy

argemone munita
poppy   2-5'
conspicuous on sunny
hillsides and in dry
disturbed areas

Grass of Parnassus

parnassia palustris
saxifrage   1-2'
graceful flower of
foothill meadows
and marshes

Meadow Rue

thalictrum fendleri
buttercup   3-5'
a tall graceful
guardian of
moist streambanks

Buttercup

ranunculus alismaefolius
buttercup   1-3'
a first plant to
flower in high
wet meadows

Sulphur Flower

eriogonum umbellatum
buckwheat   4-16"
brightens dry slopes
of open low
valleys

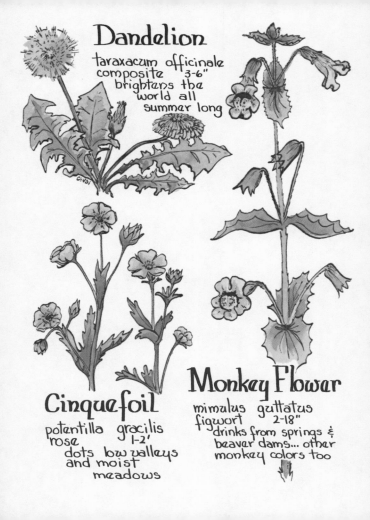

Dandelion

taraxacum officinale
composite   3-6"
brightens the
world all
summer long

Cinquefoil

potentilla gracilis
rose   1-2'
dots low valleys
and moist
meadows

MonkeyFlower

mimulus guttatus
figwort   2-18"
drinks from springs &
beaver dams... other
monkey colors too

St. John's Wort

hypericum formosum
st. john's wort   6-24"
a large family with a
little 'cousin named
'tinker's penny'

Woolly Mullein

verbascum thapsus
figwort   2-8'
a velvet weed
that colonizes
disturbed areas

Stonecrop

sedum obtusatum
stonecrop   1-8"
a succulent mat
of rocky slopes

Golden Eardrops

dicentra chrysantha
bleeding heart   1-5'
tall yellow hearts
found in disturbed
or burned areas
at low elevations

Goldenrod

solidago californica
sunflower   1-4'
clumps of golden
sunshine in dry open
meadows

Lemmon's Draba

draba lemmonii
mustard   1-5"
a ground cushion of
gravelly slopes and
in rocky crevices

Nodding Microseris

microseris nutans
composite   4-16"
stands like a big
dandelion in moist
mountain forests

Blazing Star

mentzelia laevicaulis
loasa   1-5'
a bright addition to
mountain roadsides &
disturbed areas

Woolly Sunflower

eriophyllum lanatum
composite   1-3'
this 'golden yarrow' indeed
has woolly stems & likes
dry open spaces

Balsamroot
balsamorhiza deltoidea
composite   1-3'
   clumps of yellow
   with a leaf like an
   arrowhead

Wyethia
wyethia mollis
composite   1-3'
   called 'mule ears'
   because of large
   velvety   leaves

Arnica
arnica cordifolia
composite   8-24"
   heart shaped
   leaves of
   shaded woods

Blackeyed Susan

rudbeckia hirta
composite   6-24"
a hardy bloom of dry
places & roadsides

Cone-flower

rudbeckia californica
composite   2-6'
a showy flower
scattered through
mountain meadows

Sneezweed

helenium bigelovii
composite   1-3'
colors wet mountain
meadows all through
the summer

Common Madia

madia elegans
composite 1-3'
 likes dry slopes...
 closes from mid-morning
 until mid-afternoon

Butterweed

senecio integerrimus
composite 1-3'
'groundsel' or
'ragwort' has
many relatives

Rabbitbrush

chrysothamnus nauseosus
composite 2-3'
 this late bloomer
 thrives on poor soil
 where others cannot

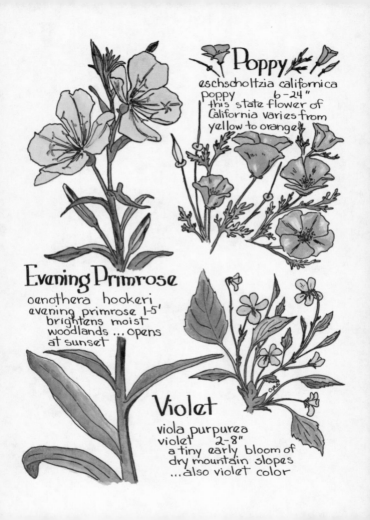

Poppy

eschscholtzia californica
poppy   6 - 24"
this state flower of
California varies from
yellow to orange

Evening Primrose

oenothera hookeri
evening primrose 1-5'
brightens moist
woodlands ... opens
at sunset

Violet

viola purpurea
violet   2-8"
a tiny early bloom of
dry mountain slopes
...also violet color

Fiddleneck

amsinckia intermedia
borage   1-3'
    an early spring trumpet
    brightly blowing over
    fields of the foothills

Wallflower

erysimum capitatum
mustard   1-3'
beautiful shades
of bright yellow
and orange

Alpine Lily

lilium parvum
lily   2-5'
    a 'little leopard lily'
    that stalks wet
    streams & swamps

Giant Hyssop
agastache urticifolia
mint   3-6'
a tall 'horsemint' with
a strong fragrance
along mountain roads

Fireweed
epilobium angustifolium
evening primrose   2-7'
sympathetic to fire
scarred areas...
many uses the
world over

Swamp Onion
allium validum
amaryllis   1-3'
a familiar odor in
wet marshy places

Yellow Throated Gilia

linanthus montanus
phlox   4-24"
'mustang clover' roams
the gravelly slopes
of the lowlands

Geranium

geranium richardsonii
geranium   1-3'
a weed that dots
shady streamsides
and wet meadows

Farewell to Spring

clarkia williamsonii
evening primrose 1-3'
heralds the coming
of summer in dry
open fields

Miner's Lettuce

montia perfoliata
purslane   4-12"
    danty saucers eaten
    by early settlers &
        miners

Lewisia

lewisia pygmaea
purslane   1-3"
    a tiny little thing
    named for Lewis
(of Lewis & Clark)

Bitterroot

lewisia rediviva
purslane   3"
    Montana's state
    flower. blooms early
    & does indeed taste bitter

Milkweed

asclepias speciosa
milkweed   2-4'
a fragrant plant
with milky juice
in stem & leaves

RosyEverlasting

antennaria rosea
composite   2-24"
woolly 'pussy toes'
that mat a variety
of habitats

Pussy Paws

calyptridium umbellatum
purslane   2-10"
fussy mits that hug the
earth early morning & eve
but upright to noonday sun

Rock Fringe
epilobium obcordatum
evening primrose 2-6"
a mat peeking
out of rocks
and boulders

Owl's Clover
orthocarpus purpurascens
snapdragon   4-16"
an early flower
that blankets
grassy fields

Sargent's Campion
silene sargentii
pink   1-5"
sticky-haired 'catchfly'
opens late in the day
on high rocky slopes

Bleeding Heart

dicentra formosa
bleeding-heart 8-18"
little broken hearts with
lacy leaves hide in moist
shady woodlands

Mountain Laurel

kalmia polifolia
heath   4-12"
a mat of evergreen
that dances round
high country lakes

Steer's Head

dicentra uniflora
bleeding-heart 1-3"
tiny big horns that
bloom briefly near
the melting snow

Manzanita

arctostaphylos patula
heath   a shrub
an evergreen with
green apple berries
& leathery leaves

Wild Rose

rosa woodsii
rose   a shrub
prickly thickets
along open
streambanks

Shooting Star

dodecatheon jeffreyi
primrose   1-2'
little comets that shine
in meadows & moist
conifer woods

Indian Paintbrush

castilleja miniata
figwort   1-3'
many colors &
  varieties

Primrose

primula suffrutescans
primrose   6-12"
  a majestic high altitude
plant that blooms thru
  the melting snow

Mountain Heath

phyllodoce empetriformis
  heath   8-20"
an evergreen shrub
found in wet places
... often mats rocks

Elephant Heads

pedicularis groenlandica
figwort   8-24"
   clumps through
   bogs & meadows
   of open spaces

Indian Pink

silene californica
pink   6-18"
a 'catchfly' with a
sticky stem in
wooded foothills

Mountain-Sorrel

oxyria digyna
buckwheat   6-12"
prefers shady wet
places on rocky
slopes & ledges

Fuchsia

zauschneria californica
evening primrose 1-2'
a bright spot on dry
rocky ridges in late
summer

Scarlet Gilia

gilia aggregata
phlox 18"
trumpets in dry
patches from
foothills to
timberline

Mountain Pride

penstemon newberryi
figwort 6-20"
"beard tongue" is a low
woody mat creeping over
boulders on roads & trails

Roseroot

sedum rosea
stonecrop   4-10"
 flat succulent leaves
 and a rose fragrance
 of moist rocky places

Snow Plant

sarcodes sanguinea
heath   4-12"
 blooms with the
 melting snow of
 the deep forest

Pinedrops

pterospora andromedia
wintergreen   1-3'
 lives off the organic
 material in the soil
 underneath the pines

Flax
linum lewisii
flax   6-24"
known for the
tough fibers
in its stem

Baby-Blue Eyes
nemophila menziesii
water leaf   4-12"
a small early
spring saucer
of the lowlands

Blue-Eyed Mary
collinsia torreyi
figwort   2-8"
tiny 'blue lips' carpet
moist sandy flats
and roadsides

Lungwort
mertensia ciliata
borage   1-5'
dangling buds of
pink turn blue
& fade again
to pink

Bluebell
campanula prenanthoides
blue bell   10-20"
delicate bellflowers
chime in shafts of
wooded sunlight

Harebell
campanula rotundifolia
blue bell   8-20"
this 'bluebell of
Scotland' rings late
into the fall

Jacob's Ladder

polemonium pulcherrimum
phlox   2-12"
a small plant with
leaves like a ladder &
a bad odor if picked

Sticksaad

hackelia jessicae
borage   1-2'
tiny "forget-me-nots"
with prickly seeds in
mountain meadows

Sky Pilot

polemonium eximium
phlox   4-12"
a hardy, musky bloom
found on high
alpine ridges

Bull Thistle

cirsium vulgare
composite   2-5'
full of thistle-down
to tinder your
campfire!

Anderson's Thistle

cirsium andersonii
composita   2-4'
elegant summer blossoms
that grace many a
mountain roadside

Phlox

phlox diffusa
phlox   4-12"
low showy mats that
brighten rocky and
sandy slopes

Lupine
lupinus latifolius
pea   1-4'
little 'quaker bonnets'
thrive in moist
mountain meadows

Chinese Houses
collinsia heterophylla
figwort   6-24"
springtime pagodas of
the foothills in open
sun or dense shade

Vetch
vicia americana
pea   2-4'
a climbing vine
of low grassy places

Salsify

tragopogon porrifolius
composite   2-4'
   like a big ripe
   dandelion with round
   white seed heads...
      also yellow

Blue-Eyed Grass

sisyrinchium bellum
iris   4-16"
   a large family of
   little 'eyes' peeping up
   from open grassy slopes

Wandering Daisy

erigeron peregrinus
composite   6-30"
   a small showy 'fleabane'
   of moist meadows
   and streambanks

Iris

iris missouriensis
iris   1-2'
   a 'blue flag' of
early summer that
likes wet places

Meadow Aster

aster alpigenus
composite   2-16"
   this little 'alpine aster'
is common in high
boggy places

Sierra Saxifrage

saxifraga aprica
saxifrage   1-5"
sturdy little heads
that sway in high
mountain meadows

Blue Dicks

brodiaea pulchella
amaryllis   1-3'
this wild hyacinth often
the first spring flower
of the lowlands

Grass   Nut

brodiaea laxa
amaryllis   1-2'
'Ithuriel's Spear' has
a nutlike bulb favored
by the Indians...
found in dry heavy soils

Sierra Gentian

gentiana holopetala
gentian   2-16"
a little cup of gentian
violet in wet mountain
meadows

Sally

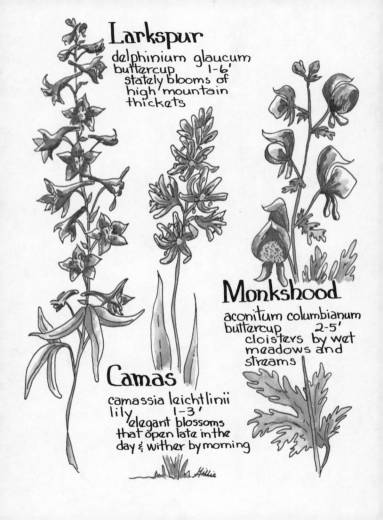

Larkspur
delphinium glaucum
buttercup   1-6'
   stately blooms of
   high mountain
   thickets

Monkshood
aconitum columbianum
buttercup   2-5'
   cloisters by wet
   meadows and
   streams

Camas
camassia leichtlinii
lily   1-3'
   elegant blossoms
   that open late in the
   day & wither by morning

flowers drawn by...

Dedication...
     to **Ivan**
who makes every
trail a 'happy day'

references...

Horn, Elizabeth L.
<u>Wildflowers 3.</u>
Beaverton, Oregon:
The Touchstone Press,
1976.

Munz, Philip A.
<u>California Mountain</u>
<u>Wildflowers.</u> Berkeley:
University of California
Press, 1963.

Niehaus, Theodore F.
and Charles L. Ripper.
<u>A Field Guide to Pacific</u>
<u>States Wildflowers.</u> Boston:
Houghton Mifflin Co., 1976.

Niehaus, Theodore F.
<u>Sierra Wildflowers.</u>
Berkeley: University
of California Press, 1974.

Orr, Robert T. and
Margaret C. <u>Wildflowers</u>
<u>of Western America.</u>
New York: Alfred A.
Knoph, Inc., 1974.